To Nate, love mom
Christmas 2019
For you to see the
Danish Hygge in
all of your world.

Llamas ~

Striped Pears and Polka Dots

Striped Pears and Polka Dots

THE ART OF BEING HAPPY

KIRSTEN SEVIG

THE COUNTRYMAN PRESS

A division of W. W. Norton & Company

Independent Publishers Since 1923

This book is dedicated to
Mike & Else Sevig,
my adorable parents.
I love you!

Hello, lovelies!

My name is Kirsten Sevig and I am an artist from Minneapolis, Minnesota. This little book is a mixtape of my illustrations, a few simple recipes, pearls of wisdom, and musings about what makes me happy. Painting is one of the greatest sources of joy in my life and it plays a big part in my daily routine and self-care. I carry a journal and a portable watercolor set wherever I go.

When it is gray and rainy, I paint myself sunshine. When I'm feeling sad, I paint in bright colors to cheer me up. Painting calms me when I am feeling anxious. When I'm overwhelmed, I make a series of small decisions about what to put on a blank page and begin to feel empowered. I often paint in public where I am in good company, but when I want to be alone, I retreat to paint at home or out in nature. I started this practice while living in Iceland. I moved with my partner-in-adventure to Reykjavík for two years starting in 2013. I had an amazing time exploring nature there, but I also experienced very difficult struggles with anxiety and depression.

I'd struggled with anxiety and depression for years, but this time I was so anxious that I wouldn't even leave my apartment. I sought help. I saw a therapist named Ólafía who taught me some big lessons: to measure success differently, focus on time over results, make potentially bad meals, and designate a time to worry, just to name a few. I am sharing the wisdom that I learned from her that was really helpful to me. Maybe it could be helpful to you, too. She taught me to shift my focus from trying to be perfect and successful to enjoying the act of creating art. I started very simply, painting on blank pages to see if I could make it up as I went, without sketching or planning, and this has become my process. I scheduled time every day to paint, and I shared my process and my thoughts on Instagram. This supportive community brought another layer of joy to my practice, allowing me to connect with like-minded people and artists across artificial boundaries. It was only by learning what I could contribute and how I could share that I was able to foster this type of meaningful exchange. It is my hope that this little book will be a portable happy place to remind you of the nuggets of happiness that can be found all around you. Always remember to take the time to do something that makes you happy!

Kirsten ☺

My Ladybug Friend

This painting will forever remind me of a tiny visitor that dropped by my striped studio one sunny morning. I had painted red dots on this page and I wasn't sure whether I should make them into berries or ladybugs when I noticed a ladybug on my window. That was a simple decision to make! I started adding legs and dots. Then she started to stroll across my painting. She found a finished ladybug and circled it over and over again. Eventually she flew back to the window and I finished this painted pattern, but I kept smiling about this visit from my new ladybug friend.

I like to ride my bicycle...

In a car, I'm in my own little bubble, a comfortable barrier from the outside world where I can control the climate and the soundtrack to my commute, and disconnect from the neighborhoods I pass through and the people I pass by. On a bicycle, I feel more alive, more present, and more connected. I notice things that I would never have noticed otherwise. Consider biking to someplace you normally drive to—not only will you get some exercise, but you also might gain a new perspective on your neighborhood!

Popcorn is one of my very favorite foods, and I make myself a giant bowl of it almost every night. I often have the intention of sharing it, but it is apparent that I just can't help myself and I eat nearly all (if not all) of it! Making popcorn on the stovetop is like performing a magic trick and witnessing one at the same time. Even though I know how it works and I can see how it is happening, it still amazes me that tiny kernels of corn become puffy white clouds of yum! Here is a recipe for popcorn on the stovetop so you can try it out yourself.

Popcorn

Ingredients:

- 3 tablespoons high smoke point oil
  (I use refined coconut oil)
- ½ cup of popcorn kernels
- Seasonings (see below)

Instructions:

1. In a covered saucepan over medium-high, heat the oil and 3 test kernels until they pop. Spoon them out.

2. Add the remaining kernels, shake to coat, and cover.

3. Remove from heat for 30 seconds.

4. Return to medium-high heat, shaking occasionally, until popping slows to 1 or 2 seconds between pops.

5. Pour into a bowl to season and serve. If you have a big bowl with a lid, you can use it to shake up your popcorn with some fun seasonings. Here are some that I like:

- *olive oil + fine sea salt* *sugar + salt (powdered in a blender)*
- *dried rosemary + dried thyme + olive oil + sea salt*
- *olive oil + sea salt + nutritional yeast flakes*
- *chaat powder (found at your nearest Indian grocery store)*

It is
still
possible
to be
completely
entertained
by a
collection of
old buttons.

Pears are the cutest.

Pears have the cutest shape. I mean no offense to all the other cute fruit out there, of course, but I just happen to prefer pears. Pears are curvy and bulbous, and their stems only add to their aesthetic value. Also, I painted a striped pear without realizing there really is such a thing, only they have a few vertical racer stripes, not horizontal stripes like this one. Keep your eyes peeled for striped pears!

THE WISDOM OF ÓLAFÍA

Focus on time, not results.

This advice felt counterintuitive, but as an antidote to performance anxiety and perfectionism paralysis, it really helped me! Decide how much time you can dedicate to your pursuit, schedule it, and stop when you have put in your time—regardless of whether or not you are finished or even like what you've done. Consider yourself successful for showing up and putting in your time. Progress takes time, as well as patience and discipline, but just focus on the time.

Bright Pants Day

I have fond memories of Bright Pants Friday at an amazing job I had a few years ago as a balloon designer. Yes, that job is a whole other story and a different illustration altogether, but my point is that you can make an ordinary day really memorable and fun if you get a bunch of people to work together while wearing brightly colored pants! It's completely arbitrary, of course. It could just as easily be hats or shirts or stripes or plaid. Just a bright idea that I think you should take and run with, if you haven't already done this.

Colorful Houses

I developed a deep appreciation for colorful houses and rooftops when I lived in Reykjavík. I befriended the darkness, wind, and rain when I chose to focus on the colorful houses on my walks through town. I think people who paint their houses colorfully do so as a public service. Perhaps they know the happiness that comes from seeing bright and saturated colors, and they are just doing their part to help lift spirits.

Rain or Shine,
there's always
a rainbow
of rooftops
in Reykjavík.

Rain Boots

When I got my first full-time job, I celebrated by buying myself a pair of knee-high, shiny yellow rain boots. Ever since that day, I have been looking for chances of rain, and imagining the possibility of puddles so I can wear them. When I moved from Minnesota to Reykjavík, rain was frequently in the forecast, which meant that I wore my yellow boots almost every day. I really loved that about living there.

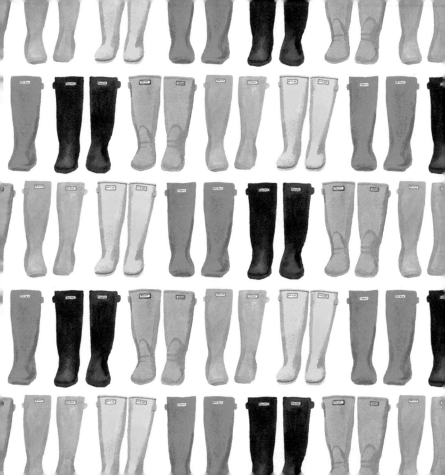

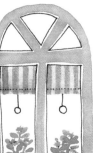

Window Displays

In the winter in Reykjavík, I noticed a trend that made me very happy: People created little displays in their windows for others to enjoy as they walked by. It was clear to me that they were meant for passersby because things were intentionally facing outwards. There was poetry to read, glowing resin lamps of animals or mushrooms, and framed pieces of art to create little galleries. In this way, I felt like they were creating sunshine in the darkness of winter for people like me. My first big purchase was a resin duck lamp so that I could reciprocate this joy.

One day, when I was missing Iceland, I doodled these expressions of Icelanders after I had smiled at them.

Icelanders usually only smile at people they know. After smiling at strangers in Reykjavík and getting strange and puzzled looks back, I began to understand. Because I look like I could be Icelandic, and Icelanders only smile at people they know, when I smiled at these strangers I think they were trying desperately to figure out how they knew me.

 *Goats!*

Goats are curious, incredibly nimble, and super cute! As I painted these goats I was reminded of Skittles. I once saw an ad by someone who was looking for a new forever home for a housebroken, well-behaved goat named Skittles. She came with a collection of colorful hand-knit sweaters she liked to wear. I wanted to adopt Skittles so badly, and so did everyone else who saw that ad. Every once in a while, I wonder about Skittles and hope she found a fantastic forever home.

I love collections
because you can pick
out your favorites.

"David Attenborough" your life.

If you are not already familiar with Sir David Attenborough, make a date to watch *Planet Earth* and marvel at the natural wonders of this amazing planet as narrated by this amazing man! Ólafía is the first person I've heard use his name as a verb. It was her way of explaining how to observe the world without judgment and approach everything with curiosity and compassion, just like Sir David Attenborough.

Dapper Dachshunds

I have had an affinity for dachshunds ever since I was little. Anytime I see a dachshund, my day is made. If they are wearing a sweater or jacket, my excitement is likely audible. And if the dachshund is being walked by an elderly mustached gentleman wearing a hat and a tweed coat with elbow patches, be still my heart! That happened once, years ago, and I will never forget it. Seriously. It was perfect!

Cats know how
to make themselves
comfortable.

Follow their example
and find yourself
a cozy spot.

Happy Glasses Day!

Who remembers the day they got their first pair of glasses? My dad does. And who would celebrate such a seemingly mundane event? Our family would, and with gusto! Every year our family celebrates this important anniversary: Glasses Day. We bake a cake and decorate it with eyeglasses, have a nice dinner with some family friends, and we have special glasses-themed cards and gifts for him, as well as an assortment of his favorite sweets. It is never too late to start a new tradition, or to create a silly holiday! What will your next celebration be?

I get a kick
out of putting
a beret
on a bird
like Eugene here.

Plants

Being in the presence of thriving plants is a wonderful way to recharge, especially when the weather is dreary. Visit a greenhouse, a conservatory, a plant nursery, or even just a local plant store. Breathe in all that fresh oxygen. Notice a plant that you have never seen before, because inevitably there will always be at least one. Marvel at the diversity of shapes, patterns, and colors. Stop to smell the flowers and the fresh herbs. Take a picture or two, or if you like to draw, paint, or read, try doing so in the company of plants.

Because we could all use more hot pink on our plates...

Pickled Red Onions

Ingredients:

- 2 small red onions
- Juice of 3 limes
- 1 tablespoon light olive oil
- 1 tablespoon salt (+ more to taste)

Instructions:

1. Quarter onions, slice very finely, and place in a bowl.

2. Sprinkle with coarse salt and a squeeze of lime juice. Stir once and let rest for about 10 minutes.

3. Cover with lukewarm water and let rest for 10 minutes.

4. Rinse and drain the onions.

5. Add the lime juice, olive oil, and salt to taste. Mix well.

6. Cover the bowl and refrigerate. The onions will turn super pink if left overnight. (I'm often impatient and eat them once they start to turn pink, which is fine.) Taste before serving and add salt if needed. Optionally, add thinly sliced tomato and chopped cilantro leaves.

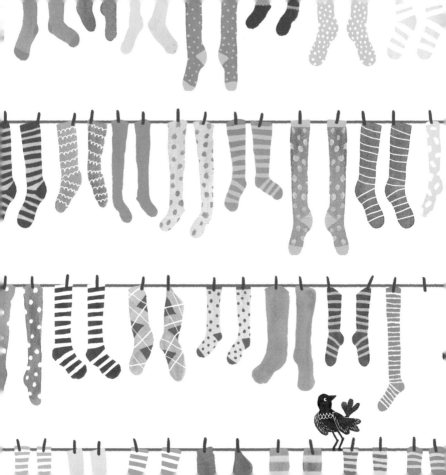

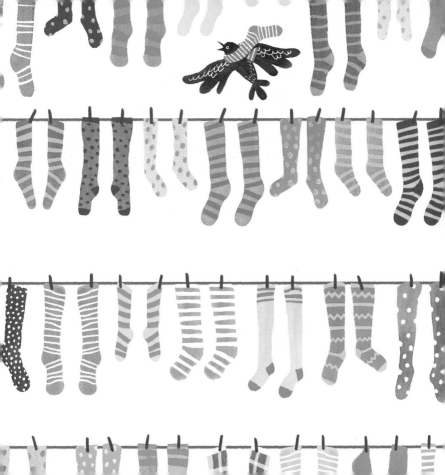

THE WISDOM OF ÓLAFÍA

Measure success differently.

Money is a trigger for me because society places so much emphasis on financial success. I felt a huge amount of pressure to be successful in this way, so Ólafía asked me to list some ways that I could measure success other than money. I decided to measure success in happiness, progress, wisdom, accumulating rejection and failure, resilience and determination, pride in my work, confidence, and comparing only to myself instead of to others.

Still Kickin' After 45 Years

When my father first met my mother, she asked him how it was going. My father answered, "It goes the way the hen kicks." This conversation took place in Norwegian, and my dad's answer was an old saying which means it isn't going well. I'm really not sure if that was his honest response or if he was just trying to impress Else, the Norwegian student. Either way, it's a cute story that we often laugh about. For their 45th wedding anniversary, I painted them these 45 hens.

Strawberry Girl

My Mormor (my mother's mother) called me Kirsten Jordbærpike when I was little, which means Kirsten Strawberry Girl, and is also an old Norwegian song. The nickname suited me well. I could not get enough of the small and oh-so-sweet strawberries we would get at the local outdoor market when I would visit Mormor in Kristiansand, Norway.

I like
making up
plants.

THE WISDOM OF ÓLAFÍA

Resilience is a skill.

This was a huge lesson for me. I had always clung to the belief that I wasn't resilient. I thought that some people were inherently more resilient, and that was just how it was. It had never occurred to me that I could become more resilient with practice, and that falling down and picking myself up again was just one way to do that. Learning this made me more emboldened to try, because even if I failed, it could help me to become more resilient.

Memorable Birds

I'll always remember painting these birds. I was in Rochester with my parents, waiting at Mayo Clinic before my mother's lumpectomy. I passed the time by painting these birds, which entertained us all. Before my mom went into surgery, I asked her if there was anything I should add. She thought I should paint feathers on their heads. While she was in surgery, my dad and I went to a coffee shop. I ordered a chai, and finished this silly piece by painting the funny feathers on top of their heads. The surgery was a success, and these birds will always remind me of that.

Toast Happy Hour

Inspired by Canteen in Minneapolis, MN

Ingredients:

· A toaster
· Bread from a local bakery
· A selection of delicious toppings, such as:

ripe avocado · *a selection of homemade jams* · *red pepper flakes* · *sea salt*
sprouts · *lemon zest* · *lemon wedges* · *a selection of nut butters* · *banana*
slices of ripe tomato · *thin slices of watermelon radish* · *pickled red onions*

Instructions:

Toast slices of bread to your liking, top them with your choice of toppings, and enjoy! Invite your friends and make it a new tradition. My favorite combinations are:

avocado + sea salt + lemon zest + sprinkle of fresh lemon juice
nut butter + jam (a classic NB&J) · *nut butter + banana slices*
avocado + sea salt + thin slices of watermelon radish + sprouts
avocado + red pepper flakes + sea salt · *avocado + pickled red onion*
avocado + ripe tomato slice + sea salt + sprouts

Take a Lesson from Sloths.

Sloths have such sweet faces that look like they are relaxed and smiling almost all of the time. Also, there is something so beautifully simple about how they live their lives hanging from trees, sleeping a good deal of the time, and eating long slow meals. I think we could all learn a lesson or two from sloths. Hang in there, take it easy, slow down, get your rest, and savor every bite of your meal.

Anything
and
everything
PLAID.

If you are ever drawing or painting something and you aren't sure what it is, if someone asks you, you can always say,

"It's a mushroom."

Even if it is totally wrong, there is a really good chance that there is a mushroom that looks just like that. Yet another reason to adore mushrooms.

A Potentially Bad Meal

After explaining my general anxiety about cooking, Ólafía assigned me to make a potentially bad meal. Without planning or overthinking, I was supposed to throw a meal together, knowing full well that it might be bad. I laughed, but it was really hard for me. I did it, though. We took two bites of my noodles drowning in soy sauce, drank a bunch of water, laughed, and went out to eat. I learned that it was okay to fail. Also, soy sauce should only be used in moderation.

It is so much fun
to gather
and arrange
found treasures.

Nøttekaker

Ingredients:

- 200 grams (1¾ cups) almond meal
- 250 grams (2 cups) powdered sugar
- about 3 egg whites*

Instructions:

1. Preheat the oven to 380°F/190°C.

2. Mix the almond meal and powdered sugar in a bowl. Gradually add unbeaten egg whites and mix until slightly sticky. Be careful not to add too much egg white; the dough should hold its shape but not be wet.

3. Place 24 clumps of dough onto a baking sheet lined with parchment paper. Bake for about 12 minutes or until lightly browned on top, solid underneath, and still a little soft in the middle. Cool on a cooling rack.

*To make vegan, mix 7 tablespoons of Ener-G egg replacer with the almond meal and vegan powdered sugar. Then add 4 tablespoons of warm water and knead well until sticky. Allow to rest for 15 minutes, knead again, and form into 24 balls. Bake for 10 to 12 minutes, and then cool on a cooling rack.

This is a Norwegian family recipe for nut cookies from my Mormor. She used a nut grinder to make her own hazelnut meal, but we usually use almonds because they cost less. If you aren't grinding your own almonds, buy unblanched almond meal, not almond flour. Now that I am vegan, my mother and I worked hard to make an eggless version so I can still enjoy these cookies. Nøttekaker keep best in the freezer, and they thaw super quickly. Their flavor exceeds their humble appearance by far, so don't be surprised if your friends want this recipe after trying these cookies, too.

When life gives you lemons,
zest them, squeeze them,
and get everything you can
out of them, just like life.

Bring Back Hats.

Hats are happy-makers for me! I enjoy seeing others wearing hats, and I often wear hats myself. Plus, there are so many amazing hats out there in so many fun styles and colors that the possibilities are endless. Consider donning a hat, not just for yourself, but as a public service. I know it can make my day! Once I saw a woman wearing a pea-green knitted beret while walking a dachshund in a matching pea-green knitted sweater. It was an unforgettable instance of dachshund happiness plus hat happiness plus knitted happiness, which was simply perfection!

Strong Women

I am not sure what I would do without the strong women in my life. They lift me up when I am down, support me and strengthen me, and challenge me in the best of ways to be vulnerable and to be the best version of myself. Whoever you are, strong women make for great company and are fantastic role models. We can all benefit from keeping good company, so surround yourself with amazing strong women.

I love
to hide
inchworms
in pretty
floral
patterns.

THE WISDOM OF ÓLAFÍA

Worry Time

Ólafía taught me that worries are often unsolved problems. She told me to set aside 30 minutes a day to write down my worries and answer these 4 questions:

- *What am I worried about?*
- *What is the worst-case scenario?*
- *How would I handle it if that happened?*
- *Can I do anything about it? If yes, what? Schedule it.*

This was super helpful to me! I've learned that the worst case scenario rarely happens. And when it did, I handled it much better than I predicted I would.

This recipe is not my brainchild, but I wanted to share it with you because discovering it was the biggest surprise, and the fact that you can make convincing meringue cookies out of what would otherwise get poured down the drain is magic! You likely have everything you need on hand to make them right now. I didn't add any cream of tartar, and my meringues turned out really well. Also, this is a great recipe for people with dietary restrictions. Just a note on making this vegan: not all sugar is vegan, so double check the sugar you want to use. A vegan will appreciate it!

Meringue Surprise

Makes about 60 cookies

Ingredients:

- Liquid from a 15 oz. (425 gram) can of chickpeas (salt-free)
- 1 teaspoon cream of tartar (optional)
- ⅔ cup (135 grams) granulated sugar
- 2 teaspoons extract (I use vanilla and/or almond extract)

Instructions:

1. Preheat the oven to 250°F/120°C. Line two baking sheets with parchment paper. Get out your stand mixer.

2. Beat the strained liquid (and cream of tartar, if using) on high speed with a whisk attachment until stiff peaks form, about 15 minutes. Add the sugar one spoonful at a time while beating until glossy. Then add extract(s).

3. Use a spoon to dollop even mounds of meringue onto the parchment paper. Bake for 1½ to 2 hours, rotating the trays halfway through baking. The finished cookies should be dry and firm. Cool before serving. Store in airtight containers and consume within 2 to 3 days.

Forest Floor Magic

If you, like me, enjoy discovering new things, crouch down to observe what is happening on the ground the next time you are walking in the woods. Look at moss. Find new mushrooms. Watch fiddlehead ferns unfurl. Notice how nature recycles. Observe insects scuttling about. Nature is top-notch entertainment, and the forest floor is your front row seat to watch it happen.

Hedgehogs

What do hedgehogs do when it rains? On the day I finished this painting, it was pouring rain. I had walked for blocks without an umbrella, getting thoroughly soaked. Rather than feeling upset by this, I felt alive and invigorated. I noticed how the water felt as it dripped from the tip of my nose. Once I was back inside and warm in dry clothes, I finished painting this array of hedgehogs while sipping a big cup of tea that my friend Kari made for me in her bright yellow studio. I like to imagine that a hedgehog might take shelter from the rain under a giant mushroom.

Cute Streets

I enjoy thinking about places where I've been that were so adorable I wanted to take them home with me. It might be a couple of beautiful buildings in a row; a historic district; a fun area where everyone decided to paint their houses bright colors; or a string of old shops that have been in business for generations, baking cakes, repairing shoes, or selling finely crafted hats. You probably just thought of a cute street right now and went there in your mind! You're welcome.

Autumn Leaves

Autumn contains so many of my favorite nuggets of happiness. There's chilly weather that calls for scarves and sweaters and warm socks, trees that look like they are lit from within as they change from green to yellow to red, the crunchy sound of leaves as you walk, day trips to pick crisp apples at a nearby orchard, and baking without feeling bad about heating up your kitchen. Sometimes I wish autumn leaves would never leave, but this season is all the more precious to me because it is fleeting. You have to stop to notice all the wonderful things as they are happening around you.

Llamas

Llamas make me smile. What is it about a llama that is just so adorable? Could it be the fact that they have big soulful eyes with long eyelashes? I'm really not sure. I just think llamas are adorable.

Chai

Recipe from my friend Keerthi
Makes 2 mugs of chai

Ingredients:

- 1 mug water + 1 mug whole milk*
- 2 tablespoons black tea powder
- 2 tablespoon granulated sugar
- 1 pinch of ground black pepper
- 2 cardamom pods, broken
- 1 coin of fresh ginger, crushed

Instructions:

1. Select two similar sized mugs to drink from. Place the water and all of the seasonings in a saucepan and bring to a boil over medium heat.

2. Add the whole milk and return to a boil. Cook for 10 minutes over medium heat, stirring occasionally to prevent burning or boiling over. Taste and adjust sweetness.

3. Strain over a fine mesh sieve and serve in your mugs.

* To make dairy-free chai, skip the water and simply add two mugs of your choice of non-dairy milk in step 1. I like using unsweetened almond milk.

Always remember to take the time to do something that makes you happy.